HOPEFUL ROMANTIC

HOPEFUL ROMANTIC
YUSEF ALI

Louverture Press
Atlanta, Georgia

To request permissions, contact the publisher:

Louverture Press
louverturepress.com
yusef@louverturepress.com

ISBN: 978-1-09835-888-4

First paperback edition March 2021
Cover art by Yusef Sullivan/Stuart Snider
Artwork by Zola Sullivan

Printed by Bookbaby in the USA.

FOR
PRINCE ROGERS NELSON

"Love does not begin and end the way we seem to think it does. Love is a battle, love is a war; love is a growing up."

James A. Baldwin

CONTENTS

I-DEFINITION OF LOVE

II POSSIBILITIES

III QUESTIONS

IV LUST VS. INTIMACY

V-AWAKENING

HOPEFUL ROMANTIC

I
DEFINITION OF LOVE

Art

Art is a celebration of the soul.
It is the innermost voice manifesting
through all beautiful things we create;
whether music, poetry, sculpture, dance, or painting
created by body and mind,
or art of love created by the heart.

I Love Life

I love life.
It hurts
me above and beyond
anything else.

'Cause I love life the way I do,
I hope for the very best
even though
I know there are times
where life will be the very worst.

Hidden in the shadows
are my visions and experiences.

Despite all the sorrows and all the hunger,
I can always count on
these visions and experiences
to bring me to something beautiful-

not to blue sky or to ocean shores
but, to a clearer understanding
of who you are and who I am,
then for a solitary moment,
I know what heaven feels like.

Love Lesson

We love each other
and love loves us,
only because
we do it so well.

Even though we have not
made love,
the world will be jealous
when they find out
all the while
we had the best recipe.

When we make love,
it will last longer than those minutes, or
hours, we once spent.

Love will be like the weeds in my backyard
I spent all day trying to get rid of.

Love will never go away.

We will make love on a bed of flowers

and love will ascend from our bodies
forming a rainbow.

Arthur,
the kid down the street
will point to the sky and yell:
"look mommy!"

Tears rolled down his mother's eyes
as she whispers inside,
"daddy and I don't make those rainbows anymore."

One day she will teach Arthur,
love means more than chasing rainbows,
it also means making it in from the rain.

Love will always love us,
because and only because,
we do it so well.

Love and the Changing Season

Seasons change and rearrange,
but love is always in season.

Tides turn on the vote of chance.

Evenings always seek out romance.
This moment I ask you, my beauty to
dance.

In our garden, roses burst from fertile seeds.

Hearts in undying love supply their needs,
unencumbered by life and all its weeds.

There will always be something between
you and me.

At this moment
it is difficult to see.

This is the call for my devotion to you.

You could not imagine a love so true,
although some say it will make you blue.

I only know of a love forever running deep,
even if my soul shall weep.

For the sheer desire to have you near,
I ask of you, my heart, bend your ear.

Moonlight and stars shall be our own.
I will only dream of you when I'm alone.

My heart truly, never rests,
and none shall receive greater tests.

Our fellow comrades are equal to the task.
If they take this very moment to ask:

Shall we take a walk through forever?

Time or distance, cannot sever, our ties,
knowing in our hearts is where the power truly
lies.

II
POSSIBILITIES

Imagine

Imagine us in our purest moment,

if forgiveness is somehow stifled.

My mouth is often partial to silence,
for emotions held close at heart.
Accept me wounded, imperfect.

Imagination,
my only redeeming quality
leading me to your door.

Fear succumbs to our experience,
complete as we are as two;

I become less than one, imagining
life without you.

Shoreline

May I lay at your shoreline?
It is the place for me.
I am yours and you are mine.
Nothing left but for us to be.
I hear your voice against the waves,
next to you feels more than fine.
For you are the lover who gives
and never saves,
lay me to sleep at your shoreline.

Focal Point

When I touched your hand,
light shined through me
like a prism bright through all sides.
I am grateful for what happened then,
but even more grateful for what happens now,
and hope it finds us one step closer to happiness.

Interlude

-Lesson:

You are always deserving, but not always
ready.

Elayne

As bees wander
to honey,
I turn into
your soft gaze
easygoing as a wave,
as butterfly wings
subtly dance into a blooming flower.

We seize a moment
lovers own,
woven into dreams,
of angels,
wistfully gliding
into a new day.

An invitation
into soft kisses
sees us
off on our journey
filled
with bliss, joy
and comfort,
knowing you
return to me,
and I,
to you.

Though the days
stretch us apart
our hearts beat
in timeless rhythm
rich in hope,
pure and vast.

We rest assured
wherever we are,
together,
is where
we will always be.

Faithful Wish

Our love is sacred
not perfect.
It is present in soft
and simmering kisses.

You take my hand
in care of our dreams, waking
each day to love anew.

If by some cold winter,
or some blistering summer,
our love crashes and fades,
I will seek your smile
and hang onto words
wrapped in your gentle breath
calling for me to love you.

Rose

When I'm put up in my bed,
she's the song in my head.
When I close my eyes
she's the song I realize.

Wandering this close;
I suppose…I suppose,
she's my rose, my rose.

Her love is my lullaby;
a mellow moon
hanging in the sky.

Our love once wrong,
now we belong.

She will never leave my sight,
now it is alright.

Her laughter it glows.

I suppose…I suppose.

She's my rose, my rose.
With her next to me,
I am more than free.

Dreaming in rainbows,
I see her smile, it glows.
I suppose…I suppose,
I am more than free.

Interlude

-Meditation:

Ok
Its
You and me
You and me
You and me

Lighthearted

I have no care
to settle up
or down.

I want to be around,
under your blanket
and out in the sun.

I was not meant
for everything or everyone.

With you,

I'm sunbaked, and cooled
by your smile
tickling in its ease
to find me.

High Ideals

Your smile colors
outside
my
fault
lines.

When reckoning moonlight reaches
the
cracks
left
unfilled,

levee may give way
to
tremor,
and
flood.

You will not stand between,
but will point me to the
splendor.

Lost and Found

The best part
of me
is the love
I give to you.

It is a home
your kindness
carved
out in me.

It begs
nothing of you
and stands
on your whims.

It raises our masts high
when we are lost
and folds them low
when we are found.

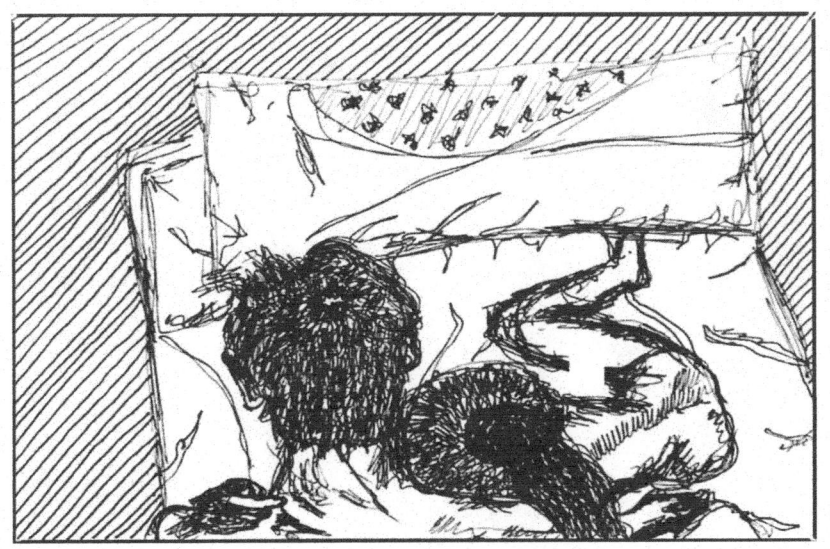

INTERLUDE

-Lyric:

As long as you speak from the heart there will always be
songs.

Cardinal Morning

I love you,
indiscriminately,
though
the season
finds it
objectionable.

My heart
is strengthened
because
I've seen
too much of you.

Your
essence
remains,
with my
steadfast
love
in its keep.

No luxury
exists
since I
held you
and silently
gazed
into your eyes.

Scent of
juniper
will not soothe me.

Course
of
persimmon
and
chantilly cream
cannot
comfort me.

A fountain
of ale,
nor rye
shall rinse
my memories
of you.

Silk sheets
woven in
Marrakech offer
no covering
like
your scent.

I am not beguiled
by
fresh
blossoms
of lilac.

Breath of dragons
could not
extinguish
my affections,
only light
the hills
and valleys
back to you.

Your
hymn
sings
through
the bubbling creek,
sorting
its way
through
a fog-tinged
moonlight
until dew
meets sunrise.

It is this cardinal morning,
I wake to feel your
heartbeat
underneath lace, skin and kisses.

A Morning East

Waking next to you
sends my morning gold,
when I can taste the pulp
of your lips and caress your hair
as it cascades to feather
our nipples.

The bell of your
words ring clear,
as you love me in circles
never getting me dizzy enough.

Rebirth

Your honesty and
Beauty ARE REAL.
Let yourself feel it.
Show up as you are.
I don't say things to "have" you.
I tell you things, so you feel safe.
If you feel safe, you feel open.
If you feel open,
you might take a chance.
Nothing will burden you.
I will come to you uncertain,
not knowing how open you are,
until you show up again,
being more of who you are
since the last time,
and granting me
the privilege to witness.

III
QUESTIONS

The Love in Question

Love does not reject or offend.
It is our greatest savior,
although I lay restless
with a more familiar notion
regressing to the mean,
drifting far from home,
praying for the courage
to ask if I can be yours.

I Wrote Love a Letter

I wrote love a letter
asking if she would keep me brave
and disprove the myths I found
in my briny sea of mind.

She responded reluctantly
and washed out my sanguine deeds.
Her words pushed against the gulls
as they preyed on my wishes
and turned them to stone.

I wrote love a letter
to give me pause
and contest what seemed blue.
She left me beguiled and forlorn.
Dashed with despair,
I sat with my questions
inviting a new premonition
voided by doubt.

I wrote love a letter,
wholesome, divided
accorded with contradiction,
slipping from my lips,
easing me toward hope,
simple and familiar
found in you.

A Second Guess

You can't trade love for rent
just because your money is spent.
And I can't be your one and only
when you are feeling lonely.
Love never comes for free
but in love, you are free to be.
Maybe there is truth in Gods timing,
no matter what, I want to keep climbing.

My heart is at your door,
beating for so much more,
although it is afraid to knock
and worried as I race the clock.
Is our love endangered, in taking time?
Or does patience bring something more sublime?

I Can't Wait for Her

I can't wait for her.

Can't wait for her to show.
Can't wait for her to know,
how far I'd go.

It's her I want to know.
Can't wait to tell her so.

Let's reveal what I feel.

Why
try
or even deny?

Rely on fate
to settle
on reasons why?

It is not up for debate,
though I relate.

You can't see what I feel.
Let's reveal what I feel.

What's inside
I can't hide.

How could you go
and not even know?

Fragile

I entered as a wanderer
to find her place inside.
Climate and terrain changed.
The crosses we carried
lessened in weight,
fixing my unsteady hand.
Unlikely partner I suppose,
but I wonder where the time goes.

Hunger Strike

I write of you
while you're away.
My heart's appetite grows for you,
because I cannot feast.

I know not of your return,
nor when my heart will
break free of you
and end its hunger strike.

Misplaced

The morning hours have come again.
A few jazz tunes, carry the bittersweet sound of yesteryear
as an irony of bright light looms overhead.

My body longs for comfort
only found in company of old friends,
or is it I fail
to realize a greater void within?

I fight to transform consciousness
in preparation for another emotional filter,
unless I can convince myself there is a reason
in you granting me wings to soar far beyond this room
absent of a lover's touch.

Only occasional sighs manage
to break the silence after the music stopped.

A prayer is overdue to resolve what I thirst for.

In times like this, matters of the heart
are a war, men long to win,
but cannot begin to fight,
when they have placed
their happiness in the hands of another.

Ladybird

May I stay for what you fancy?
Is it love
passing me by,
in the collage of your sky?

Last Call

Swimmingly my heart is on edge
as I shift into your autumnal gaze.

I feel misplaced in your heart's journey
by some postulate urge sitting behind
your eyes.

Sipping scotch in our twilight, my heart
beats out of rhythm and ahead of its
time.

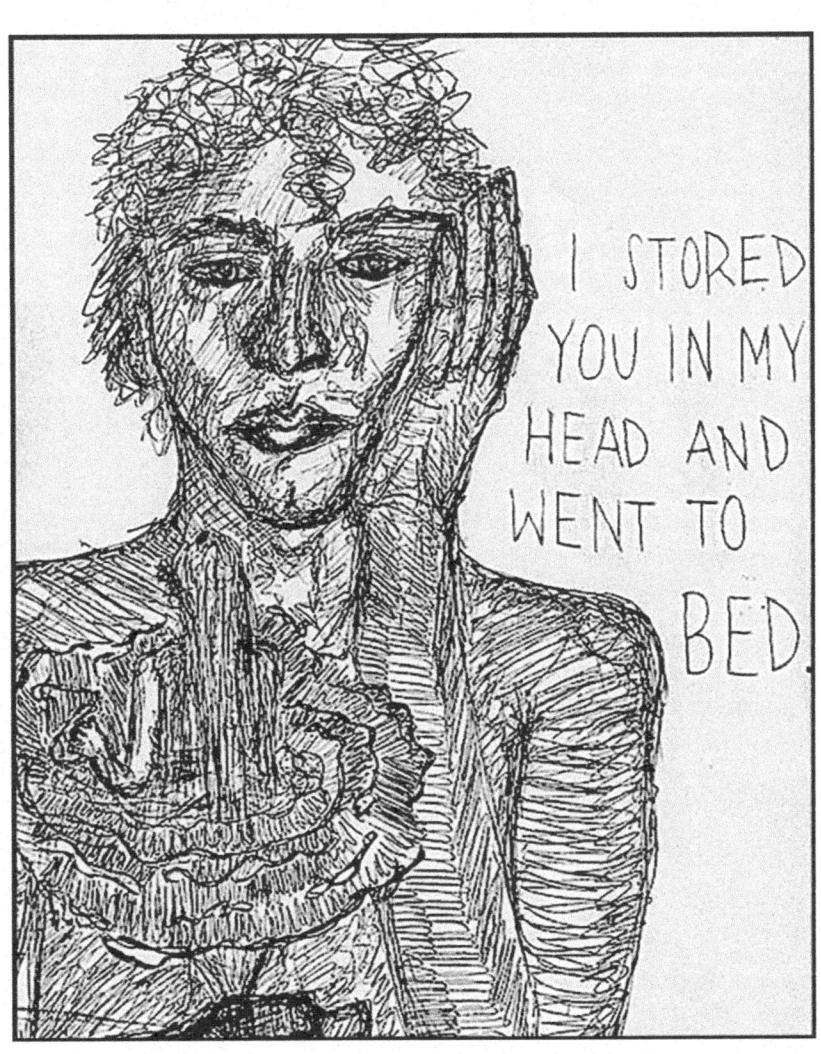

IV
LUST VS. INTIMACY

Vintage Ebony

If there were anything perfect
it flashed through her skin,
especially her
darker parts.
Hair and nipples
were pleasure chambers.

Her eyes
wore the
light of her mind,
confirmed the truth
fed from her lips,
and the sweat of her skin
so I could discover myself.

Fangs

White teeth
entitled to a healthy portion,
speak from a need in me
to discover within her,
undulating tides, woven into her flesh.

I imbibe her wishes
as her fingernails clench,
I unfurl her wings
smooth, and ornamental.
Bright as if, she bloomed
turning outward, and angelic,
her pursed wings
meeting mine.

We hunger for freedom,
contained underneath her skin.
I administer to her, as I suck,
to taste, is to travel deeper.
Her wrists coiled beneath my fingers,
as her blood pools about my tongue,
swallowing her divine affections.

She chides and chuckles.
For pleasure she does not compete.
It is hers to give or receive.
In her satisfaction, she screams a song of him,
her flesh always welcome to the whims,
fashioned only in his fangs.

Unguarded

Vulnerable and beautiful,
we turn infinite
boiling in ecstasy,
whether we stand or lay.

Our bond is free.
We effervesce,
pleasure full of
grace and plunder.

Sordid measures
weighed in moans and sweat;
trading potions
as pieces of gold
spun from nirvana.

Deluge

She takes me places
when she is not present.
Together, we endeavor
to well-lit spaces.
She needs to know,
I know,
we both saw darker places,
we no longer go.
We go there
to special places,
deep and low,
so deep and low.

Majesty

When
we flowered,
our magic door
flung wide.
Clasped hands and
bright eyes,
brought out
the stars, steeping
in our breasts
as I adorned
a new universe in
you.

INTERLUDE

-Reflection

The rain came and reminded me of the soft,
plump kiss I left at a friend's place.

Clandestine

I took your whispers with me
when they dripped
on the hairs of my neck
and slid recklessly about my follicles
to tuck themselves
under my skin.

They bathed in me,
and I bathed, in each of them,
to record in my memory
until the tape ran out.

Rewound and replayed-
in between our foray
and the unknown,
until commanded
by your urge.

I aim my hunger
toward your breath, again,
willing to wait
for it to travel back
to me, whether a fortnight,
or forever.

Textures

In word and deed my love has
no restraint to nurture
and provide.

It is the light, nectar and water
of every flower.

It is the here and somewhere
stretching
beyond the heavens
and around your waist.

Love is my protection
when you forget
what to wear,
but you will remember,
where we were
when my fingers
shivered through your hair,
and I descended to your edge,
to decorate, and warm you
with no courage.

Dust

Our meeting is narrative of baptism,
though I emerged
from your fantasies.

As you held me firelit in your eyes,
our story began like paper set adrift
from a rickety desk,
and finding its way
across the uneven floor,
by way of the box fan,
gathering dust and dander.

As the light of the moon
shoved its way through the windows
and dingy curtains,
it ushered a more heavenly dust,
to refine the broken hearts
we failed to scrub
from underneath our nailbeds.

You cannot cleanse what you long to mask.
There is no longer a nemesis forcing its
way in between us.

All we know, we will soon forget
about the dust we bring,
the dust we left behind
and the dust underneath
our clothes on the floor.

Loving Free

I heed the chime in your breath,
hoarding its timbre.

It was rustic and unpolished
like a barn door hidden in high cotton.

We courted from the field and loosened
pangs fueling fire in our blood,

where the backdraft silently burned

and untangled orchid
tendrils blooming of beating hearts.

Still in the breeze and easy acres
we disappeared although,

we opened our eyes and grew soft in the sun.

These dreams resuscitate all
that died from the love
I kept inside
and never set to fly because
I wanted to know your wings.

V
AWAKENING

Unpacking (A Four-Part Disharmony)

self-protection:

I gave up my art
which was unwise,
because I kept myself from you
and our relationship
became a product of secrets

temptation:

Infidelity
as an intervention
of incongruence

forgiveness prerequisite:

What if instead of blamed, I apologized to my lovers
for not knowing how to love them and refusing to
learn how?

enlightenment:

Embracing the feminine

Expansion (Daises Under Moonlight)

Love is a unique touch,
incomparable
to what we knew.

Love is guided
by a force unseen
without, and within.

Daises were not born under moonlight;
love was never made by hand.
The universe is ever-expanding,
and love is the light of a distant star
traveling to shine on you.

Redemption

I refuse to be a prisoner of my past,
or be a victim of a love I could not make last.
I shall not worry about the why and when.
Nothing remains of way back then.
I only hope to live again,
and put to rest the burdens of sin.
In suffering, we gain
the lessons standing behind our pain.

Unlearning Toxic Masculinity

There is nothing artisanal
about emotions.
Perhaps I am wrong.
I as others
hasten to single them out,
as profound and profane.
Men are taught to question emotions.

How could we erase them?
Can we take away their breath?
Why let them live in us?
Because if they survive,
how could we?
Were they not born to shame us?

I hope to grant my emotions clemency,
and end the practice of breaking my
heart open with bare hands
to find the love inside.

A Fresh Start

Many a breakup is permission to love yourself for the
first time; inquire within.

"It's all about falling in love with yourself and sharing that love with someone who appreciates you, rather than looking for love to compensate for a self-love deficit."

Eartha Kitt

NOTES

James A. Baldwin quote reprinted from
Nobody Knows My Name: More Notes of a Native Son (1961)

ACKNOWLEDGEMENTS

God, the ancestors who guide and nurture me, Mom, Dad, Nikki, Rab, Isaiah, Elijah, Zola, Linda, Brenda, Jim, Skip, Tina, Mac, Debbie, Penny, Erica, Zoey, Rubye, Dow, Kirk, Louise, Christian, Kelly, Ty, the Whatleys, the Hyatts, the Taylors, the Worthys, the Toatleys, the Vaughns, Erica, Elliott, Heather, Caren, Tre, Amanda L., Craig, the Stanbacks, the Holts, the Harris family, Eric V., David, Free, Daphne, Les, Mari, the Downeys, the Daughertys, Mark and E., Deb and K., Jason, Greg S., Omar, Latoya, the Briscoes, Drew, Lisa H., Phen, Steve, Danny, Marcelle, Maceo, Carolyn P., Lori R., Erin, Cal, George, Mary Moore and my CW fam, Matthew, KK, Stu, Lauren M., Mary W., Peter C., Myka H., Jamie, Stefanie, Tony, Catherine, Lly, Larry S., Monte, Andre D., Mike J., Kirk C., Rayshon, Henry, the Davis family, Lisa R., Rachel, Indra, Bob, Rob, Doug, Jill Smith, Cozy Shawn, Ausar, Daz, Mary Frances, Dejoun, Tyrone, Jay, Kebbi, Willis, Morgan, Rob, Quinton W., Terri, Pat, Charisse, Cal, Atiba, Tiffany, Brett, Bailey, Margy, Adrienne, Mary C., Skinny Lisa, Chris, Conrad, Gianni, Pep, Pam, Wayne, Carolyn, Kisha, Tabatha, Daronte, Charisse, Ryan, Daana, Tangee, Maria, Jean-Claude, Matt W. and Melissa A.

Special gratitude to my artistic inspirations:

Toni Morrison, James Baldwin, Langston Hughes, Bruce Lee, Pablo Neruda, Khalil Gibran, Malcolm X, Roxane Gay, Bell Hooks, Brene Brown, Esther Perel, Muhammad Ali and Nayyirah Waheed.

Special dedication to the shadow artists, the artists here, and the artists yet to be born.

ABOUT THE AUTHOR

Yusef Ali was born in the Atlanta area known as the "SWATS", coined in the mid-1990s by recording artists, Goodie Mob and Outkast out of appreciation and respect for their Southwest Atlanta neighborhoods.

After graduating high school, Yusef remained in Atlanta and worked his way through college to earn a Bachelor's degree in Accounting from Georgia State University.

During college Yusef began writing poetry, exploring love, race, art, politics, nature and society. Yusef was a regular of the Atlanta open mic poetry scene during the mid/late 1990s, and hosted poetry events at the Red Light Cafe, Patty Hut Cafe and Club Esso.

As the 1990s ended, Yusef married, became a father, leaving the open mic poetry scene behind to focus on family and career. Yusef worked in Finance for ten years, before making a transition into the Culinary Arts/Gourmet Retail industry working as a Retail Manager, Culinary Instructor, and Barista.

While working as a Barista, Yusef rediscovered his passion for writing poetry. Hopeful Romantic is his first book, under independent publishing imprint, Louverture Press, named for Haitian revolutionary, Toussaint Louverture.